Managing Your
Stress

WAYNE E. OATES

Managing Your Stress

Philadelphia

E BIBLE COLLEGE

The "Social Readjustment Rating Scale" and the "Frequency Distribution of Life Changes During 10 Years Prior to Hospitalization
for 199 Patients" are reprinted from *Separation and Depression*, John
P. Scott and Edward C. Senay, eds., AAAS Pub. No. 94, 1973. Used
by permission of the American Association for the Advancement of
Science.

Biblical quotations, unless otherwise noted, are from the Revised
Standard Version of the Bible, copyright 1946, 1952, ©1971, 1973
by the Division of Christian Education of the National Council of
the Churches of Christ in the U.S.A. and are used by permission.

Library of Congress Cataloging-in-Publication Data

Oates, Wayne Edward, 1917–
  Managing your stress.

  Bibliography: p.
  1. Stress (Psychology)   I. Title.
BF575.S75O23   1985   155.9   85–13123
ISBN 0–8006–1880–7

1776D85   Printed in the United States of America   1-1880

Contents

Introduction

What Is Stress?

Stress, strain, tension, pressure, demands, or even "anxiety"—these are old words we use to describe how we feel when the limits of our strength and energy are being tested severely. Hans Selye, the pioneer in stress studies, says that stress moves through a three-stage process when it comes upon us. First, our whole system goes into a state of alarm. Second, our system mobilizes our emotional, spiritual, and physical stamina to resist stress. The third stage is the exhaustion of those resources. Earlier studies of stress led many to believe that stress is really the aging process and that depleted resources are nonrenewable. However, more recently we have become less and less convinced of this gloomy outlook. We are concentrating on ways of increasing stress tolerance, of finding means to renew depleted resources for resisting stress, and of learning new skills for managing stress. That is what this manual is all about.

— 1 —

Understanding
Stress

One of the most important ways of managing stress is to have a clear understanding of it. We have the most trouble bearing meaningless stress. Is *all* stress bad? This is the first question to ask. The answer is no. Stress is like heat in your body or in the engine of your automobile. Some of it is vitally necessary to the proper functioning of your body or your car. Too little or too much is equally threatening. An effective balance must be maintained.

Selye makes an important distinction between *eustress*, good stress that you invite, seek out, revel in, and enjoy, and *distress*. Examples of eustress are participating in an athletic event, organizing a party, deciding to become and then actually becoming a parent, and producing any work of art, literature, or scientific discovery. Creativity has its unique kind of stress. Selye speaks of *distress* as the kind of stress you avoid, dread, and suffer when it comes upon you. One example of distress is the loss of a loved one by death, divorce, separation, or estrangement. Other examples are failing in school, losing a job, becoming seriously ill, facing military combat, and confronting death. Less dramatic examples of distress are boredom, conflict on the job, marital or family quarrels, or the accumulation of bills or debts that you cannot pay.

I prefer to make a distinction between necessary and unnecessary stress. Some stresses, like going to work in the morning, doing a competent day's work, caring for those we love when they are in severe trouble, are necessary stresses. In an earlier time, I can remember such stresses were known as duties. But, the word duty has more recently been infused with a negative connotation. Nevertheless, to call one's agreed-upon duties "necessary stresses" may make them not only easier to bear but sound better as well. Another way of looking at necessary stresses is to see them as the common lot of all responsible human beings. To ask to be excepted from them is to ask to give up a part of what being human is all about.

Yet, there are unnecessary stresses that truly complicate being human. The sexual harassment of women—or men for that matter—while they are trying to get an ordinary day's work done is an unnecessary stress. In business and personal affairs, those who avoid making simple decisions that would enable other people affected by those decisions to get on with their lives produce unnecessary stress. To quibble about the letter of the law until the very intention of the law has been violated is an unnecessary bureaucratic stress. Very subtly, then, the issues of good and bad stress bring to the surface the imperatives of justice toward and love for our neighbors.

The Bible gives us some helpful understandings of stress. Biblical teaching, when received steadily and holistically, gives remarkable perspective to the meaning of stress. No one word in the Bible is translated as stress, although the word "distress" appears often in English translations of the Bible. However, several words *mean* stress.

The first of these words is affliction. Paul speaks of afflictions in 2 Cor. 1:3–7. The God and Father of our Lord Jesus Christ comforts us "in all our affliction, so that we may be able to comfort those who are in any affliction, with the comfort with which we are comforted by God." Bearing stress and receiving comfort from God equip or enable us to be comforters to others. Notice how much more help comes to you from those who have been through similar afflictions. They help you manage these stresses.

Paul also uses the word suffering to describe stress. He says that suffering—or stress—can build up rather than tear down your personhood because of your faith in Christ. "Suffering," he says, "produces endurance, and endurance produces character, and character produces hope, and hope does not disappoint us, because God's love has been poured into our hearts through the Holy Spirit which has been given to us" (Rom. 5:3–5).

The human spirit *does learn* to tolerate more and more stress through self-discipline. The athlete's stamina is increased by practice, by scrimmaging, and by becoming a veteran player. Soldiers, sailors, and marine or air force personnel are subjected to intensive survival, evasion, resistance, and escape training to prepare them for combat duty. Medical students, interns, and residents are subjected to long hours of duty and are called upon to serve people in desperate struggles for their lives. The committed pastor has gone through years of study and discipline in the basic meanings of the Bible, the history of the Christian churches, the substance of Christian doctrines, ethics, and practice. The discipline helps when it is time to put the training to practice.

You can increase your capacity to withstand stress by facing rather than fleeing from those who have been through similar struggles. You can lighten your load of stress by refusing to act as if you are the first and only person to have something like this happen. You are a very special and beloved person in the mind and heart of God. Yet, you are not, thereby, an exception to the thousand mortal ills the flesh is heir to and the slings and arrows of fortune that affect our common lot as human beings. No, you are showing signs of honesty and humanity to admit that you are under stress. You participate in God's chosen destiny for you when you seek to master it rather than be over-whelmed by it.

Other words for stress in the New Testament are burden and load. In Gal. 6:2 we are urged: "Bear one another's burdens, and so fulfill the law of Christ." The law of Christ is that we love one another as he loved us. We fulfill this law when we form a spiritual covenant with one another to share our part of the weight of the common lot of human stress—losses through death, desertion, divorce, and alienation; ca-tastrophes such as fire, flood, famine, and war; human fault and weaknesses in which we overtake, confront, and forgive one another. These are community stresses, affecting the body corporate of all of us together and not just each of us separately.

Then, in Gal. 6:5 we are told: "For each man [or person] will have to bear his [or her] own load." These are stresses that each person carries for himself or herself. Earning one's own bread is one of them. Tak-ing care of one's own health is another. So is dem-onstrating one's competence to perform responsible and unique service in one's own right. This acceptance of legitimate personal stress might also mean we can-not assume that one is simply to be waited on hand and foot by one's marital partner. Paul put it another way in 2 Thess. 3:10: "If anyone will not work, let him not eat." Although work is not the center of the gospel, the laid-back avoidance of its stresses is not to be rewarded. We are, by the nature of the work many of us do, losing the value that comes from the exertion of the big muscles of our bodies. We live in even temperatures all year around and never sweat. The absence of the strain of toil, the sweat of the heat of the day, the stretching of muscle, tendon, and nerve produces a kind of stress of its own in that we do not carry those parts of the load that are ours. I was recently in the home of a physician who enjoys finding, cutting, and furnishing the wood with which he totally heats his house. He said that it makes him take a warm place more seriously and less for granted. It reduces his stress from his daily work as a neurologist. Remarkably enough, his young wife also enjoys baking their bread herself. For her, it is a diversion from instructing mentally retarded children all day.

A final New Testament word for stress is one that is often translated as temptation. In other places it is translated as trial, or to put to the test. Martin Luther translated the word into the German word *anfechtung* which means stress, anguish, testing, trial. Thus, we could pray the Lord's Prayer: "Lead us not into stress, times of testing, trial, or tribulation, but deliver us from evil." These times of testing can be developmental: leaving home for school, work, or military service or retirement from a job. They may be times of grief: the death of a loved one, divorce from a spouse, the loss of an extremely significant job, or a severe episode of mental illness. Such times of testing may be catastrophes that affect multitudes of others: a hurricane, a tornado, a riot, a war. To be delivered from such testing, to have survived it, to have come through it, is to live with awesome gratitude for having been delivered. Note, however, that catastrophic stresses which involve others create a community of sufferers. On the other hand, divorce, job loss, or severe mental illness tend to isolate a person from others. In a sense, then, these isolating stresses are harder to bear and certainly are not surrounded with the drama that inspires public sympathy.

Another word for stress in the Bible, especially the King James version, is straitened. Jeremiah speaks of Judah and Jerusalem being in a "siege and straitness, wherewith their enemies, and they that seek their lives, shall straiten them" (Jer. 19:9). The Revised Standard version translates the Hebrew word *tsug* as distress and/or afflict. The apostle Paul picks up the thought and uses it to say to the Corinthians that they are restricted, literally "short-breathed," in their affection for him. Jesus speaks of the impending end of his life on the cross and says "how I am straitened (or constrained) until it is accomplished."

These points of view are probably the most important factors for you to consider about your experience of stress: How long will it last? When will relief come?

How much longer can you stand it? How much more can you take? Where is your exhaustion point? In World War II men were in combat "for the duration." Getting wounded, getting captured, deserting, or becoming ill were the only possible ends. In the Vietnam War, men knew that if they could stand being in a combat zone for a specific length of time—365 days in the instance of the Army or 395 days in the Navy or Marines—the war would be over for them. Yes. Someone else replaced them but *they* could go home. As a result, during the months of combat in Vietnam there were three times fewer neuropsychiatric casualties than in World War II.

Therefore, if you can decide how long you plan to endure the stress you suffer, then you can endure it with more serenity, and less friction within yourself and between you and your colleagues, family, and friends. You need not even announce this decision. Simply act on it. This is one of the first principles about stress management.

A final interpretation of stress rests in the words for pain in the New Testament. The word translated into pain is *ponos* and it has a double meaning. First, it means hard labor or toil. Zeus brought a utopian state of affairs on earth to an end and sent *ponos* into the life of man. Jehovah God, in expelling Adam and Eve from the Garden of Eden, told the man that he would work "in the sweat of your face" and woman that she would have "pain in childbearing" (Gen. 3:19, 16). In Col. 4:13, the word *ponos* means "worked hard." Little wonder is it today, then, that we inevitably associate hard work with stress. In the increasing number of reports on workaholism or work addiction, the element of unremitting, uninterrupted stress is always described.

However, this word *ponos* is also translated as pain. Pain is spoken of as undergoing hardship and the New Jerusalem is spoken of in Revelation as the time when there is "no more death, mourning, crying, or pain." Here it seems that some aspects of hope in mankind hinge on the removal of stress, pain, and suffering. Hence, we tend to see much stress as bad, counterproductive, and to be "gotten through."

On the other hand, though, some pain is looked upon as creative, as being gladly endured because of the joy of the outcome. Examples of this are the rigor and stress of childbearing in which the mother is doing her most creative act. Similarly, Jesus is depicted in Heb. 12:2 as the one "who for the joy that was set before him endured the cross . . ." This kind of stress is the Olympic stress of ancient Greek athletes who deliberately stressed themselves to try to win the trophies which lay ahead of them.

The word self-discipline is a quaint word in our vocabularies today. I am not suggesting that stress be managed by simply grinning and bearing it or by lifting yourself by your own bootstraps. To the contrary, I am saying that you can absorb more and more stress by using practice and discipline to learn new sets of habits. You can increase your resistance to the alarms that stress creates. You can become the *user* of stress rather than its victim through personal devotion and learning stress management skills. You can learn to practice the arts of meditation, prayer, and health-conducive breathing, and to make useful diversionary behaviors a part of your technique for using stress.

— 2 —

Stress Management
Abilities

Now that we have developed some understanding of what we mean by the word stress, we can begin to identify some of the abilities it takes to effectively manage the stress that you have to handle each day, week, month, or year. Whenever you improve these abilities, you reduce the stress you have to bear or manage it more easily, effectively, and creatively. You could just as easily call them capacities as abilities. Through self-discipline and consistent practice, you can increase your capacity to do the things I am about to suggest.

The Capacity to Make Decisions

Much unnecessary stress arises from the constant fretting, avoidance of responsibility, and frank fear of the unknown that reflect our indecisiveness. This is like having a sore that will not heal. You approach a difficult decision and then back away from it. Some

psychologists call this the approach-avoidance syndrome. Some call it choice anxiety, that is, anxiety in
the face of having to choose between or among a variety of unsatisfactory alternatives. Regardless of what
it is called it doesn't lead to bliss, happiness, or ease.
B. F. Skinner says that decision-making enables you
to escape from an aversive or stressful condition to a
state of feeling free of threats of coercion or restriction
of your movements, of comfort and of thinking. In this
sense stress becomes the eternal vigilance lest that
freedom be taken from us again by indecision. Skinner
says that one way human beings can bring indecision
to an end is by "announcing" their decisions. You tell
your close friends what you have decided: to marry,
divorce, become a Christian, go to college, quit your
job, or change jobs. This announcement may take
courage, but it does commit you, more or less.

Such observations, however, do not consider the evidence of how snap decision-making, impulsive action
without prior thought, can forfeit your freedom, trap
you in severely negative consequences, and thereby
multiply your stress. Decisions that are the product
of impaired judgment don't reduce stress either. Persons who are severely depressed are likely to make
very dangerous decisions such as selling all their prop-
erty, spending money prodigally or, at worst, attempt-
ing or actually completing suicide. They do this to
bring some kind of stop to the severe pain of their
inner turmoil.

Therefore, there are polar extremes in decision making: the procrastinating dawdler who never can make up his or her mind and the severely disturbed person who is likely to make quick, foolish, and even life-threatening decisions.

Between these extremes is the person who methodically goes about making decisions. He or she arrives at a reflective rather than an impulsive decision by a process simple in concept, more difficult in execution.

First, collect all the information or data you need about the decision you are trying to make. If you cannot find all the facts you need, then you can decide when and where and how you can get this information. You put the matter aside and quit fretting about it and stressing yourself until you find the data. To decide that you cannot decide now and to determine a time when you will decide relieve the stress you bear and the confusion you have to tolerate. This is known as patience!

Second, you can seek consultation from other knowledgeable people about their know-how in dealing with the problem you have at hand. Other people who have successfully weathered such a stress are often, though not always, the wiser for it. Some can mark out guideposts for you in your decision-making. They can both warn and console you.

Third, you must take into consideration the outer limits of time, energy, money, and other resources you have for making this decision. Time is the most neglected of these limits. Sometimes procrastination causes the decision to be made for you through default. Therefore, the careful use of time is necessary for effective decision-making.

Fourth, consider the promises or covenants you have made. Ask yourself how your decision is already shaped by those covenants. My approach to ethical decision-making requires that I not make any new promises at the expense of any already established promises. Maybe these older covenants can be renegotiated. But if not, fidelity requires that they be kept ahead of other, more desirable, ones.

Furthermore, I have found that stress always increases when someone places a demand upon me and does not make a reciprocal commitment of any kind to me. People may, for example, write to me asking me to spend a week of my time, travel 2,000 miles, and work all day, every day, for them. Yet, they do not tell me where I will sleep and eat while there, how often I shall speak or lead conferences, whether they will pay my expenses, or whether and/or how much they will pay me for all of this effort. To agree to their request would be to make a one-way covenant. Such a covenant always produces far more stress than two-way, reciprocal covenants. In brief, stay out of one-way covenants and you will have less stress. This is especially true of long-term relationships such as marriage or jobs. Unless a balanced I-thou relationship filled with a mutual understanding is thought out, then the chances of the marriage or the job aborting are very high.

Then, too, in some of these relationships, the understanding may have been very good ten or twenty years ago. Now, new growth calls for a new covenant. Are both partners willing to make a new covenant? Are they hardened by past experiences so that they want things the way they were at the beginning? God made and makes new covenants with us. This is God's way of loving us as we grow. God expects us to be brave enough to make new covenants with one another.

Finally, when you have made a decision and put it into action, do not second-guess yourself. You have put your hand to the plow. Don't look back and wonder if you have done the right thing. This "rag-chewing" of decisions already made is another futile source of stress. When I do this in my conversations with my very wise wife, she listens tenderly and patiently. Then she says, "You did what you saw to be best at the time you did it. If you were at the spot exactly again and knew what you knew then, you would do the same thing again. Quit fretting about it." That is the wisdom I would pass on to you. One of the greatest sources of unnecessary stress is the kind of rumination I call second-guessing yourself. Cattle rechew their food for digestive purposes. The only reason for rechewing a decision already made is to make it work better in each application, to etch it more deeply in your memories, and to tighten up the efficiency with which it works. If a decision repeatedly fails to work, then a total reassessment is needed. But usually this is not the case. More frequently the decision requires us to leave a significant portion of our history behind us to accomplish new things in life. We mourn this. Yet do not let mourning become a way of life for you. Grieve, but have done with grief, too.

The Capacity for Frustration Tolerance

A considerable part of the management of stress is shaped by your capacity to tolerate frustration. Popular speech has a good phrase for frustration: being stymied. Seemingly immovable obstacles are found, have fallen, and are put in your way. You are "up against it." Dollard and Miller many years ago traced anger, aggression, hostility, and rage to experiences of frustration. Pitirim Sorokin described social conflict and catastrophic stress such as riots, revolutions, and wars as the result of the mass frustration of basic human needs for food, places to live, and gainful work to do.

One of the truly important abilities you need is a tolerance for frustration; however, it is even more important to know your own boiling point better than anyone else does. Thus you can anticipate your frustration tolerance point, back off from your stress, and take a break. Every good baseball pitcher exercises his right to step off the pitcher's mound for a few seconds to collect his composure when he is about to be rattled. So should you!

The Capacity for Tolerating Ambiguous Situations

Life is not a set of clear-cut choices. Work and home situations are always far from perfect. Rarely do we find a political climate that is free of incompetence, some dishonesty, and much mediocrity. Yet, in all these situations *something* makes them worthwhile. Selye speaks of the earliest phase of stress as being an "alarm reaction." He further states that an organism cannot stay perpetually in a state of alarm. Nevertheless, you and I can look back on periods in our lives when we were constantly alarmed and upset. All our resources were at what the Navy calls general quarters, a time on a ship when every person is at a battle station ready for the most extreme action. If we find that the workaday world puts us in this state, one reason may be that we can't put up with something that is less than perfect, less than clear-cut. As tough as it may be to accept, the workaday world is full of ambiguity. This means that situations admit of more than one interpretation. Faint, ambiguous shadows fall on our most dogmatic assertions during our interaction with others. Reasonable minds under these circumstances will tend to think, "There are more ways of looking at this issue than you say." Of course, we need to balance our acceptance of ambiguity. We don't want to spend forever equivocating and letting any one issue "die of a thousand qualifications," as T. S. Eliot put it. Nor do we want to be caught or catch ourselves offsides by deleting all the possible understandings of a stressful situation except one. Have more than one hypothesis. Test them all.

The Capacity to Target Your Anger Accurately and Wisely

Frustration generates anger. Your management of stress depends on your capacity to "target" your anger toward legitimate recipients and to use your anger wisely. Otherwise you are the slave of indiscriminate bursts of anger and blind rage. Your management of stress can be indexed or measured by the size and significance of the issues it takes to "get your goat," to "tee you off," to cause you to "lose your cool." Yet, if you can take careful aim and focus the amount of temper to fit the size of the thing or issue which stimulates your anger, then your expression of anger may well be one creative way of managing stress. It may come as a surprise, but you are the one who decides how much it takes to cause you to fight back. As Kenny Rogers puts it, *you* know when to stand and fight (and

I would add, for what you will stand and fight), and when to walk away.

This seems easy as I describe it, but it calls for reflection, prayer, and personal self-control to target your anger accurately and wisely. Under stress, three reactions are possible—fight, flight, and playing dead. In other words, you fight back, you walk away, or you act as if nothing has happened. All three of these responses take energy. All three of them activate the biochemistry of the body. Peter Bourne, for example, identified the "stress steroid" that builds up in the body, called 17-OHCS. He and a research team measured this substance through laboratory tests of excretions from American combat personnel in action in Vietnam. It was demonstrated under field conditions that the various levels of the stress steroid found were indicative of "an individual's characteristic style of dealing with day-to-day stresses" (Peter Bourne, *Men, Stress, and Vietnam*, 19–23). The build-up of 17-OHCS is manifested by cumulative fatigue which is greater than that which occurs from simply being tired due to negative stress-free activity. Helicopter medi-vac crews, Green Berets in action, and other groups of combatants were studied.

In civilian studies, the relation of stressors as precursors of illness, to which reference will be made in detail later, is further corroboration of this evidence.

The fight-flight-playing dead responses are patterned along the habitual ways a person targets and uses—or fails to target and is victimized by—his or her own anger or perception of threat in his or her world. Therefore, when you find yourself being "heated up" by a given set of circumstances, you can to some extent determine just how stressful you intend it to be to you. You can decide how seriously you intend to take it and whether you are going to let it bug you slightly, very much, or to death as we put it in our slang.

Your Sense of Purpose in Life

What you are up to in the world, what you consider most worthwhile, whose estimate of you you value most highly, and the deepest commitments you have in life are different ways of describing or defining your purpose in life. This specific sense of purpose is the basis for making judgments about your responses to stressful stimuli. Small things can become stresses to one person that another person with a clear-cut sense of purpose would be too preoccupied to notice.

Hence, we arrive at the foundational capacity for coping with or managing stress: having a clear-cut sense of purpose in life. Paul described this when he said, "Slight momentary affliction is preparing for us an eternal weight of glory all beyond comparison"

(2 Cor. 4:17). The yoke of responsibility and the burden of its stress are easy when you have a clear-cut sense of purpose. The very state of being without a purpose in life creates distress in its own right. The parents of a twenty-five- to thirty-year-old son or daughter who seems to be without stress, simply drifts, is laid back, and seems to feel the world owes him or her a living are stressed and, in turn, place stress upon the son or daughter in increasingly heavy conflicts. A person who would seem to be burdened with enormous stress, yet who has a specific purpose in life, such as starting a business from scratch, can tolerate huge quantities of stress because his or her efforts are goal-oriented.

What we are talking about here essentially is the relation of morale to stress tolerance. The unemployed person who is also skilled and knows his or her purpose for living is massively stressed from the frustration and thwarted purpose of unemployment. Recently, the term burn-out has been used to describe a working person's having reached the exhaustion stage of the general adaptation syndrome of stress. It is used further to describe a collapse of the worker's sense of morale. I would prefer to sum these up in terms of the frustration or loss of sense of purpose on the job. Some workers will put it plainly: "When *they* instituted *their* new administrative structure, they cut the heart out of my reason for being on this job." Burn-out, then, is a term like love; it covers a multitude of bureaucratic sins. Management by morale is a rarely mentioned administrative way of doing things, but it deserves consideration in management approaches to work stress.

— 3 —

Spread Your Stress
Load

You do not have full control of all the stress events that occur in your life. You do have control over some of the stresses that happen to you. You can spread some of them out by putting more time between the stressful events.

Thomas Holmes and Minoru Masuda conducted an extensive stress study in an effort to find out just how many and how severe were the stressful events that occurred in the lives of a selected group of persons just before each came down with an illness. They assigned a certain "weight" to each of forty-three events. (You can tell that this work was done in what is now another era by looking at the sizes of the mortgages they mention in evaluating financial stress!) They concluded that if the number values of these weighted events at a given time totals over three-hundred, one is at risk of or highly susceptible to becoming ill in whatever way one may be prone to become ill. The list of events and the weight given to them is seen in table 1.

TABLE 1
Social Readjustment Rating Scale

Rank	Life Event	Mean Value
1	Death of spouse	100
2	Divorce	73
3	Marital separation	65
4	Jail term	63
5	Death of close family member	63
6	Personal injury or illness	53
7	Marriage	50
8	Fired at work	47
9	Marital reconciliation	45
10	Retirement	45
11	Change in health of family member	44
12	Pregnancy	40
13	Sex difficulties	39
14	Gain of new family member	39
15	Business readjustment	39
16	Change in financial state	38
17	Death of close friend	37
18	Change to different line of work	36
19	Change in number of arguments with spouse	35
20	Mortgage over $10,000	31
21	Foreclosure of mortgage or loan	30
22	Change in responsibilities at work	29
23	Son or daughter leaving home	29
24	Trouble with in-laws	29
25	Outstanding personal achievement	28

Rank	Life Event	Mean Value
26	Wife begins or stops work	26
27	Begin or end school	26
28	Change in living conditions	25
29	Revision of personal habits	24
30	Trouble with boss	23
31	Change in work hours or conditions	20
32	Change in residence	20
33	Change in schools	20
34	Change in recreation	19
35	Change in church activities	19
36	Change in social activities	18
37	Mortgage or loan less than $10,000	17
38	Change in sleeping habits	16
39	Change in number of family get-togethers	15
40	Change in eating habits	15
41	Vacation	13
42	Christmas	12
43	Minor violations of the law	11

(Thomas H. Holmes, and Minoru Masuda, "Life Change and Illness Susceptibility." Reprinted from *Separation and Depression*, AAAS, 1973. 161–86. Publication No. 94. From Holmes and Rahe, 1967, Table 3, 216.)

As you can well see, twenty-one of these events cluster around your family life and register changes that take place in that sector of your life. Eight of them specifically relate to your work arena and events that occur there: being fired from your work or retirement, for example. An injury or illness ranks sixth in the amount of stress it generates.

Another insight provided by Holmes and Masuda is that the frequency with which a given stress event occurs is important also. A vacation is forty-first in the amount of stress it creates but first in the number of times it occurs. Personal injury is second in the number of times it occurs and sixth in the weight it creates. Table 2 gives you this perspective.

TABLE 2
FREQUENCY DISTRIBUTION OF LIFE CHANGES
DURING 10 YEARS PRIOR TO
HOSPITALIZATION FOR 199 PATIENTS

| | OCCURRENCES | | MAGNI- |
ITEM	Number	Per Subject	TUDE
Vacation	894	4.492	13
Personal injury or illness	792	3.980	53
Change in residence	730	3.668	20
Mortgage or loan less than $10,000	328	1.648	17
Change in work hours or conditions	315	1.583	20
Change in financial state	313	1.573	38
Change in recreation	305	1.533	19
Change in social activities	279	1.402	18
Change to different line of work	275	1.382	36
Change in sleeping habits	266	1.337	16
Change in responsibilities at work	265	1.332	29
Change in eating habits	262	1.317	15
Change in health of family member	250	1.256	44

| | Occurrences | | Magni- |
Item	Number	Per Subject	tude
Minor violations of the law	245	1.231	11
Death of close friend	242	1.216	37
Gain of new family member	237	1.191	39
Death of close family member	229	1.151	63
Outstanding personal achievement	200	1.005	28
Revision of personal habits	199	1.000	24
Change in living conditions	196	0.985	25
Change in number of family get-togethers	159	0.799	15
Sex difficulties	159	0.799	39
Change in church activities	147	0.739	19
Wife begins or stops work	132	0.663	26
Change in number of arguments with spouse	125	0.628	35
Begin or end school	113	0.568	26
Marital separation	109	0.548	65
Business readjustment	107	0.538	39
Trouble with boss	102	0.513	23
Son or daughter leaving home	94	0.472	29
Mortgage over $10,000	83	0.417	31
Trouble with in-laws	77	0.387	29
Marriage	71	0.357	50
Change in schools	67	0.337	20
Jail term	62	0.312	63

| | Occurrences | | Magni- |
Item	Number	Per Subject	tude
Retirement	43	0.216	45
Divorce	34	0.171	73
Foreclosure of mortgage or loan	18	0.090	30
Fired at work	17	0.085	47
Death of spouse	12	0.060	100

(Thomas H. Holmes, and Minoru Masuda, "Life Change and Illness Susceptibility." Reprinted from *Separation and Depression*, AAAS, 1973. 161–86. Publication No. 94. From T. S. Holmes, 1970, Table III-11.)

Now that you have seen the original data of this much publicized research, let us see what we can draw out of it to be of real help to you in distributing your load of care. As the hymn puts it, you may be "weak and heavy laden, cumbered with a load of care." In addition to taking this to the Lord in prayer, you can be empowered by the Lord in redistributing or spreading out the load.

For example, if you are changing jobs, changing your place of residence and a son or daughter is leaving home, you are accumulating 85 stress points. Let us assume that you are a widow or widower and have decided to get married also. You have control over when you get married. You can decide, within limits, when you will move and/or change jobs. You can space these events if you choose. You do not have to accomplish them all within a one-month period. You can choose to take one thing at a time and do it with a degree of pleasure. Yet, I see people deliberately plan their lives so that everything happens at once. It is of their own doing.

Now, I must enter a common sense disclaimer: you and I have had stress events occur one right after another over which we apparently have no control. "When it rains, it pours!" is more than a salt company's slogan. I have seen people cope with the death of a spouse, the collapse of the family fortune, and a severe, unpredicted illness, all at the same time. Your situation is not always within your control.

Nevertheless, I am confident that stress events, more often than not, are not just the result of bad luck and catastrophes. They are the result of specific decisions we make. *We* decide when many of them will or will not occur. Therefore, we can modulate the amount of stress we absorb at a given time by getting out of the habit of coping with stressful life events at a "bumper-to-bumper" pace. We can remove some of the stress of life and bear the rest of it with more equanimity if we cease to tailgate ourselves emotionally.

Deferring the time of a job change, a wedding, a change in residence, a mortgage, or a change in church activities is very often within the range of your control. Spread such events out over a period of time. Create some lapses of time between stress events as much as possible. This will bring a measure of serenity and help you manage the stress more effectively. If the particular stress is, hopefully, a happy one (a wedding, a vacation or occupying a new house), then you can enjoy it more. It is more likely to be what Selye calls eustress, or good stress, than it is to be distress. The element of joyful anticipation is added when delight is in the offing.

An important disclaimer must be entered concerning the Holmes and Rahe Stress Scale. The weight of a given stress varies according to whether you have ever faced this stress before; frequency seems to lower the impact. You may be a novice or a veteran, for example, at grief. You may have been through several severe losses in your lifetime. Another person may have lived to be fifty or sixty years old and may have never experienced the death of a friend or loved one.

Another important modifier of the impact of a given stress event is the suddenness with which it occurs. To have had time to anticipate losing a job enables you to negotiate for another job more easily. If you succeed in getting another job, then you do not have a job loss but a job change. The stress is much less. We know that it takes longer to recover from a sudden loss by death than it does from anticipatory grief. The element of shock is escalated to the nth degree when the loss is not anticipated. The references in the Holmes and Rahe Scale to the death of a spouse, another family member, and a close friend do not account for this as such, although I am sure they would clinically assess this factor. This is not a criticism but an attempt to fine tune the use of this excellent scale.

A third observation about the applicability of the stress scale is this: specific age, occupation, and sex factors tend to change the meaning of many of the forty-three items for given individuals. For example, children have stress factors not listed here. By and large, this is an adult stress scale.

Furthermore, military families differ vastly from civilian families in the kinds of stress items. For example, when a drill sergeant is in cycle and leading a group of new recruits in almost round-the-clock training, the stresses in his family are vastly different from when he is out of cycle and has large amounts of time to spend at home. Navy personnel on a nuclear submarine may be at sea for three months and have shore duty for three months. Add to this the stresses of being in actual combat. A new scale is needed here.

Finally, the effects of the stress events of the Holmes-Rahe Scale, it seems to me, are different for men and women. A change of residence or the entry of a new person into the home (a new baby or an aging parent), may stress women in a much more intense way. On the other hand, it seems to me that retirement stresses the male more. This factor of sex differences in precipitating the effects of stress is changing because of the recent intense involvement of women in the out-of-home work force. However, the historic conventional differences between men and women cause stress events, in some cases, to have different effects.

The main point of this section, however, is to assure you that you are often both responsible for and capable of distributing your stress load. You can shift it around within certain limits. You can space controllable stress events. In this way, you become the manager and not the victim of your stress load.

— 4 —

Building, Maintaining, and Replenishing Your Life-Support System

Another major stress-management strategy is the building, maintaining, and replenishing of a life-support system of individuals and groups who sustain you and whom you sustain as you all go through times of stress. Your life-support system has several layers of caring persons. Let me identify them.

Your Intimate Friends

First, you have a few very close friends with whom you can talk openly, freely, and with complete trust. You can share times of trouble, disappointment, and hurt with them. They listen, understand, and give you the benefit of their advice. Also, when you have times of great achievement and happiness, they can celebrate with you, congratulate you, yet never make you feel that they are jealous or envious. You do these same things for them in their times of trouble or celebration. It is a mutual relationship that inspires hope and builds bridges over troubled waters. They literally go through things with you.

These persons, however, do not always stay put. They move away, they retire, they die, or they may turn against you for one reason or another—or seemingly for no reason at all. They, or you, may move up or down the social ladder and thereby get out of touch. Therefore, out of necessity, you must continually be about the task of making new friends and bringing fresh recruits into your life-support system.

Your Family

Second, your life-support system is made up of your family. If you are married and/or a parent, your spouse and/or your children are inextricably involved in the stresses you undergo. You are blessed indeed if yours is a close-knit family which keeps each other up-dated on how much stress each of you is bearing. (Basic honesty requires me to say that many families are *not* supportive of one another in times of stress. To the contrary, family members sometimes may be the cause of stress.) As you can see from Holmes and Rahe's Stress Scale, many of the stresses named are family stresses. Still, an important part of your life-support system is made up of your family members. You go through things together; you learn with each other how to solve problems, cope with stress, and grow together. The family that cannot do this, however, multiplies the weight of whatever stress is being handled.

Your Work Associates

A third layer of your support group is composed of your work associates. Children and young people have schoolmates. Older persons find comrades on the job. The ability of work associates to cover for each other, to instruct, and to learn from each other on the job enhances the amounts of stress they can handle. As I have mentioned before, job burn-out may be a catch phrase to describe the inner situation of a worker who receives little or no emotional support from his or her work associates, whose best efforts are frustrated, and whose personal needs are ignored by work associates.

Your Church

A fourth dimension of your life-support system can be your church. As in the case of the family, this is not always true. I hope in your instance it *is* true. One special feature of the church is that it is composed of people of all ages. From the womb-to-the-tomb and beyond, the church is a gathered community of limit-conscious and stress-ridden people who have banded together under the Lordship of Jesus Christ and through the power of the Holy Spirit to glorify God by performing works of love toward their neighbors. Going through stress is a big part of this banding together.

Worship in large and small groups aids in this. Being known by a specific small group in the church and being a part of its intimate fellowship provides you with people to reach out to when they are under stress and to turn to when you are under stress. Mutuality like this generates hope—and hope makes stress more manageable.

Adequate Briefing and Information

You have a right to ask, "What does a life-support system actually do to reduce stress in my life?" It does several things. When the alarm of a stress event occurs, you wonder what is happening to you. Your intimate friends, your family, your work associates, and your fellow church people can be more objective than you can. They can give you information and brief you while you are in a state of alarm. These friends can gently prevent you from making unwise decisions and tell you how such events are usually handled. For example, when a family has to place an aging and infirm parent or grandparent in a nursing home, it needs all the information and briefing possible about the kinds of facilities available, ways of financing, and the emotional and spiritual struggle involved. Should you lose your job, the same kind of care is needed.

Adequate Debriefing

Second, the members of your life-support system are helpful in debriefing you during and after severe times of stress. In stressful situations, each of you can turn to another in your support system and take turns being good listeners. Simply telling it both like it is and how it feels is remarkable at minimizing stress. This helps you to sort out the facts of what happened from the feelings that the events generated. Debriefing is a helpful part of decision-making in that you are less likely to make snap judgments on the basis of a stressed perspective. Debriefing introduces wisdom; pent-up feelings may result in folly. Talk it over with co-workers, friends, family, or fellow church members. Be sure that you do not bottle up stress within yourself.

Yet, a word of caution is needed here. Debriefing is one thing. Rehashing the same old story until you begin to sound like a broken record to your co-workers, your family, your friends, and your fellow church members escalates both your stress and theirs. You may be substituting talking about what is stressing you for doing something about it. To do something calls for making decisions; implementing those decisions may call for the courage to take a leap of faith into the unknown. Sitting, griping, whining, ruminating, and stewing in your own juices is a form of stress not mentioned in any list of stresses. This is a kind of self-generated stress. Only you can put an end to it with decisive action. Without this decisive action of your own, your life-support persons may feel that you are abusing the hospitality of their attentiveness. If they are people of wisdom and action, they want you to get on with life. They can stand, sit, and listen for only so long before you become the "same old story" to them.

I am awed, though, by the ways in which I see neighbors, friends, family members, co-workers, and church persons faithfully stay by each other, through good report and evil report, in the debriefing process. I am also deeply concerned when I see isolated persons go through a whole week or several weeks having no significant person with whom to converse. Many patients who come into the hospitals where I serve have as their primary need someone to take them and the story of their lives seriously. Let me tell you of a few groups of such persons who are handling stress in a maladaptive, self-destructive way and suggest some life-support systems for them. You may be one of these struggling persons or you may know someone like them.

Persons with Eating Disorders

Such disorders include obesity, anorexia nervosa (the refusal of food), and bulimia (the gorging of food and/or voluntary and self-induced vomiting of one's food). These persons think or feel they have been left alone—or may actually be left alone—to solve all stresses by themselves. They feel that the whole load, all burdens, and all stresses, is to be absorbed by them alone. Breaking this isolation is the first order of the day in being of any meaningful help to them. Building a trust based relationship takes time. Individual, group, or family therapy in a medical setting can be of great assistance in starting this process. A voluntary group, Overeaters Anonymous, is especially helpful to obese persons. (Look in the telephone book in any reasonably large town or city for this name and its number.) Take note of how Weight Watchers has become a multimillion dollar business and how books on dieting and nutrition tend to become best sellers. We are a nation of over-eaters and non-eaters.

Persons with a Substance
Abuse Disorder

You are aware that millions of people in this country seek to alleviate their stress with alcohol, illegal drugs, and prescription medications. The early and middle phases of these disorders begin and develop in isolation. Those in the person's life-support system either over-indulge or neglect him or her. Alcoholism and drug addiction usually push a person into a negative community, populated by other addicts, loan sharks, drug pushers, pimps, and prostitutes. These are the people who become the victim's support system. They exact a toll that assumes the person *will* be pathologically dependent upon them.

Remarkably enough, as one maxim puts it, these people have been broken by a community and they are to be healed by a community. Alcoholics Anonymous, Ala-Teen and Al-Anon are life-support communities aimed at healing these broken persons and their families. If you find yourself handling your stress by abusing drugs or alcohol, or if you have a friend or family member who does, look in the telephone book for Alcoholics Anonymous. Call. Help will be on its way. These people know how to brief and debrief chemically-dependent persons. If a physician is needed, they can get you in touch with one who sees these maladies for the diseases they are.

Bereaved Persons Who Fail To Recover or to Thrive

Grief over the death of a spouse is ranked at 100 on the Holmes-Rahe Stress Scale. Some people fail to recover or thrive after the death of someone very close to them. I don't want to diminish the impact of losing one's spouse or other close relative, but in my own observation of bereaved people, I see more profound and longer lasting grief over the death of a child. A child is, in a real way, nonreplaceable. After the funeral of the child, after the thinning of the crowd of relatives, parents are often without a life-support system of friends, family, co-workers, or church groups. Then, too, those who would be supportive at home, work, and church may have become exhausted in their efforts to console a person who refuses to be consoled.

The needs of those who have lost a child are sufficiently widespread that they have begun to find each other. They have begun a national support group known as Compassionate Friends. You can get in touch with them at: National Compassionate Friends, National Headquarters, P.O. Box 1347, Oak Brook, IL 60521. Their objective is to be a life-support group for parents who have lost children. A similar group is SIDS, for sudden infant death syndrome parents who have lost a baby in what is more commonly called crib death. They can be reached at: National SIDS Foundation, 310 S. Michigan Avenue, Chicago, IL 60604.

Formerly Married Groups

Many churches today have become increasingly aware of the special needs of persons who are divorced. Special groups are being formed in which the leader of a church meets with divorced persons to build a network of people who have been through this trauma. You may be such a person in need of support who could find a group like this by simply calling the office of a church of your choice and inquiring. You may, however, prefer to rely on the support of either an individual counselor or group therapy set in the more private atmosphere of the office of a good pastoral counselor, clinical psychologist, social worker, or physician.

The Convalescing Patient

Reentry to one's world of family, social, work, and church life after any serious illness is a form of stress undiscerned by many, if not most, well persons. A person's confidence in himself or herself is strongly shaken by a severe illness. The state of being sick makes you dependent, many times completely dependent, on others. To reenter the world as an independent and productive person lays demands on you that you cannot meet as if nothing had ever happened to you. Your family, your work associates, your church family, and your friends too quickly perceive you as completely self-sufficient. This is a lonely time for you.

The persons who have undergone heart surgery have begun to form groups of their own known as Mended Hearts. If this kind of surgery has been yours to undergo, ask your surgeon or one of his or her office staff if there is such a group near you. Try the group out and see if it is good news to you.

Those who have been hospitalized for a mental disorder have rarely been thought of as needing a period of convalescence. Yet, they definitely do need one. The medications for these patients' disorders require careful monitoring and supervision by physicians and nurses. The family of the patient needs explanations and guidance by social workers and pastoral counselors. Employers, with the foreknowledge and permission of the patient, may be advised of suggested schedules and duties for the patient's return to work. George Bennett has written an excellent book for both the patient and his or her family entitled *When the Mental Patient Comes Home* (Philadelphia: Westminster Press, 1980). I encourage you to get this book if you or a member of your family, a co-worker, or a fellow church person has recently returned from a psychiatric hospitalization.

A self-help group which is especially designed for mental patients is Recovery, Incorporated. Their address is: Recovery, Inc., 116 S. Michigan Avenue, Chicago, IL 60603.

Isolation, then, multiplies the weight of stress. Sharing with persons who care what happens to you and learning with them how to increase your resistance to stress multiply your capacity to bear the burden and carry the load. In this way, you fulfill the law of Christ that we love one another as he has loved us.

— 5 —

Interrupting and Choosing an End to Stress

Interrupting Stress

If you think of your life as struggle and combat with stress upon stress, interrupting the stress is something you *can* do, especially if you take an "I can" rather than "I can't" posture from the outset. For example, a husband and wife had three jobs — the husband had a full-time job and a half-time job, the wife, a full-time job. In addition, both of them were in school. The wife had physical problems that troubled them both. The symptoms were real, bothersome, and a burden to her. On hearing this, I encouraged them to get a reliable sitter for their children and take a long weekend vacation to a nearby city, state park, or campground. They were reluctant, but an emergency occurred and the stress they felt was so great they *had* to find a way to interrupt it. They did so with a long weekend; the physical symptoms subsided for seven full days.

Localized pain symptoms can be alleviated for as much as forty-eight to seventy-two hours by interrupting the stress system in addition to receiving adequate medical diagnosis and treatment. Consequently, I suggest that you build into your lifestyle a periodic get away. Several short, two- to three-day vacations have a remarkable way of interrupting stress, providing a family or a couple takes time to regroup with one another, to debrief one another, and simply to enjoy the pleasure of each other's company. Distinctly spiritual meaning can be given to these events. They can be retreats. A Catholic monastery, Gethsemane at Bardstown, Kentucky, provides retreats for individuals who want to pull away from their stressed lives for meditation, prayer, and the reordering of their lives. Our Lord Jesus Christ pulled himself away from his stressed life. In Matt. 14:23, after the feeding of the 5,000, we read, "And after he had dismissed the crowds, he went up on the mountain by himself to pray." Suffice it to say that his aloneness was interrupted by his disciples' distress on the sea. Yet he sought to be alone, to renew his life in solitary prayer. In 1 Cor. 7:5 Paul cites the interruption of marital relations as being generated in order that a couple "by agreement for a season" may devote themselves to prayer. Couples often stress each other to such an extent that they, as individuals and as a couple, lose touch with God. In their inconsiderateness of one another, their prayers are "hindered," as indicated in 1 Pet. 3:7. Interrupting such stress with solitude with God in prayer is a therapeutic balm on inflamed relationships.

There are at least three kinds of interruptions of accumulated stress you can use.

Rotations of Duties

One way to interrupt the stress within your day's work is by rotating out of one set of duties, out of one shift, out of one daily schedule and into another. Let me illustrate. If you are a sales manager and the stress of sales meetings begins to build up, perhaps you can rotate out of sales meetings into direct sales yourself. A teacher often finds the classroom a relief and even a refuge from faculty meetings and committees. If you are a housewife, you may find rotating from work inside the house to outside work to be an interruption of a build-up of pressure, strain, stress. I find that rotating from teaching students and treating patients to consulting with my fellow faculty members about the state of the research on a given problem to be a renewal of my spirit. I find that rotating from both of these to a time of writing to be a stress-breaker for me. Even getting to spend a whole day in the library is a luxurious stress interruption for me, though I may be intensely at work there.

Diversions

Another way of interrupting stress is with a diversion. For example, if you have debriefed your feelings about a stressful situation and have begun rehashing, ruminating, and fretting about it, you are ready for a diversion. Americans are finding walking, jogging, or running to be successful diversions. These use up the imbalances in your body chemistry produced by uninterrupted stress. You find that your fatigue drops off. Your confusion disappears. Your perception is more accurate. Your judgment is more reliable after such a diversion. Your walking, jogging, or running should be done according to a plan; remember to obtain medical advice regarding your previous habits, your present age, and your basic physical condition, especially your cardiovascular system. Then build up your activity gradually and not suddenly.

Another diversion many people use is an avocation. I know a few physicians, for example, who are also pastors of small church congregations. Another physician I know is an accomplished vocalist and sings in a Bach Society choir. Albert Schweitzer, the renowned medical missionary, was also a world authority on Bach. Yet another physician I know uses farming as a diversion from his practice of medicine. One more is an actor in regional drama productions. A minister I knew many years ago was a beekeeper and sold the honey to the surrounding community. Another minister was a gourmet cook and diverted himself from his pastoral work by gardening and canning fruits and vegetables. He gave canned goods from "The Parson's Pantry" for Christmas presents and as gifts on other occasions. Another minister is an expert horticulturist who grows roses. For me, writing *certain kinds* of material serves as a diversion. Writing the trilogy, *Confessions of a Workaholic*, *Workaholics: Make Laziness Work for You*, and *Nurturing Silence in a Noisy Heart*, was such a diversion for me. When I am asked to speak on these subjects, it is a welcome diversion from the stresses of teaching and caring for acutely psychotic persons.

I was a page in the United States Senate from 1930 to 1934 and became more than casually informed about the art and, occasionally, the science of politics. Following the intricacies of national politics is a diversion from the other stresses in my life. Sometimes—as in the case of the Vietnam War and the Iranian hostage crisis—following politics becomes an over-shadowing distraction with tragic implications. In times of relative peace, however, it is my spectator sport. In denominational and professional settings, political activity has often become a body contact sport! Ordinarily it has, even in these instances, been a source of humor, a game to play and one in which one avoids being a sore loser or a vindictive winner.

If you have not developed a repertoire of diversions to interrupt the stresses of your life, then it is imperative that you do so. The diversions will be a renewing grace to you, a source of variety on the theme of your life, and a means of interrupting the unceasing pressures of stress.

Total Rest

No amount of rotation of duties or diversion to avocational activity handles the exhaustion phase of stress. During World War II, Grinker and Spiegel concluded that operational fatigue could best be treated at a hospital unit placed as near to the site of battle as possible. The first treatment of choice was total rest in a clean bed with cooked meals and tender loving care. Seventy-two hours of this led to the remarkable cessation of many symptoms. Stress at its heaviest *is* combat fatigue!

You can locate stressful times in your life if you will observe several things. You are tired when you get up in the morning. You push yourself through your day. You make seemingly stupid, small mistakes—misplacing a tool, a file folder, or a telephone number. You begin chewing out people, especially anonymous ones—clerks at a post office or filling station attendants. You become confused. You begin to second-guess your decisions. In fact, it's one of those days you should not have gotten out of bed!

You need a day, a weekend, a week of total rest. Get it! Do not wait until the flu, the resurgence of acute pain from an old orthopedic injury, pneumonia, or depression forces you to take the rest. Whether you are a public school teacher, a nurse, an electrician, or an assembly line worker, take either sick leave or a vacation day, preferably on a Friday or a Monday. Sleep in! This means not even going to parties, to a club meeting, or to church. Do not just keep using coffee, taking diet pills, or eating excessively. Do not take muscle relaxants such as Valium, Librium, which is next worst, or, the worst of all, alcohol, marijuana, or cocaine. These simply defer the day of reckoning when stress erupts into major health problems. You are the only person capable of taking full charge of your life. If you are exhausted, follow the lead of the so-called dumb animals which lie down and rest when they get tired. God waits a long time before he *makes* you lie down, as is said in the Twenty-third Psalm.

Putting an End to Stress

Technical research on stress, ancient wisdom, and common sense all agree that stress is more easily borne if you know when it will be over, when it will end. Early Christians could survive persecution with the hope that Jesus Christ would soon come and put an end to it. That event was known as the eschaton or the end of time. As I have said before, Vietnam combat troops knew their tour of duty *had* an end if they could make it that long. They talked of getting the days down to double digits. Then the single digit day came; they developed the single digit fidgets and had to be exceptionally cautious not to "mess up" before the final day came.

In civilian life, the year itself has built-in endings—the April 15 deadline for tax payment, the end of the school year, vacation time, Thanksgiving, Christmas, New Year's, Easter. In family life, natural ends occur when the last child starts or finishes school and leaves home, when the mortgage on the house is paid off, when retirement occurs. These are endings that you simply count on; you do not have to make them happen but only must react to them and modify their impact.

On the other hand many negative stresses that have no apparent end to them beset people. The most common one is a severely stressful job. You may have a measure of security, a steady income, and good fringe benefits. You may have been at the job so long that you hang on for dear life because of the seniority and perquisites. Yet, you did not get a hoped-for promotion. You lost three fellow workers. They were not replaced. They stood it as long as they could and left. They left you holding the bag, either cutting back services or stretching yourself over duties they performed. You wonder how long you can hold out, stand it, put up with it.

Let me suggest that you seek consultation with a trusted confidant or counselor. You are too close to the situation, probably up to your eyes in it. Collaborate with your counselor to generate fresh alternatives, such as possible job openings that are available. The question is, "How long can you stand this?" Do not wait until the exhaustion phase of stress hits you when your resistance is gone. Make the decision as to when and how to put an end to the stress. You may think of your job as the whole world in itself, a sort of flat earth beyond which there is nothing—no hope, nothing but the foreboding of the unknown. But this is an illusion. Galaxies of universes are beyond. Decide when you are going to change jobs. This decision in itself will lower the stress, even if it is to make your move five years from now. If you can't make a decision, it may be that you need additional events to take place, new information that is not now available. You can decide then when you will decide. This too will lower your stress level.

A few people, and I certainly hope that you are not one of them, become so locked into impossible situations that they fall into a deep depression. In responsible people who perform heavy duties, a clinical depression tends to be part of larger political power struggles in the job and/or home. The pain of their depression can be so great that they may impulsively decide to put an end to their life. This is how desperately stressed from within and without people can get. These desperate straits represent a collapse of that person's curiosity, a reduction in his or her capacity to innovate and to form new alternatives in a severe situation, and a depletion of the energy to put any suggestion from others into effect. Such a person also suffers a serious disruption of the biochemical balance in his or her body and needs highly-skilled medical attention. The indications for immediate medical attention are these: severe loss of or increase in appetite, inability to sleep or to be refreshed by the sleep one does get, a slowing down of the ability to move freely, loss of sexual interest and ability, and recurrent thoughts of suicide. All stress-ridden persons should consult their physicians, but persons with these symptoms should go to their physicians and ask specifically for help with their depression.

From a spiritual point of view, an escape route from stress that affirms rather than destroys your life is available. You should be perplexed by your stresses but not to the point that they cause despair. As Paul puts it, "No temptation has overtaken you that is not common to man. God is faithful, and he will not let you be tempted beyond your strength, but with the temptation will also provide the way of escape, that you may be able to endure it" (1 Cor. 10:13).

— 6 —

Spiritual Commitment and Stress Management

I hope that you have sensed a theme of spiritual commitment running through what you have read so far. The awareness of the presence of God and a whole-hearted sense of purpose in life tend to offset and soften the blow and lighten the weight of stress. Hans Selye attests to the substance, if not the form, of what I have just said. He said, on one occasion when I heard him speak, "Most people can break out of the habit of being a 'race horse achiever' inviting stress or the habit of being passive 'turtle absorbers' of stress. To do this you must learn a code of behavior."

Selye's Code of Behavior

Selye suggests these principles for managing stress.

First, find the personal level of stress you can bear without becoming exhausted and counterproductive.

Second, be altruistic but take care of yourself at the same time. If you are going to serve others well, you must at the same time survive and do well yourself. Nature's model for this is your own body. All the tissues in your body are altruistic except cancer cells. Cooperate with your own tissues. The *joie de vivre*, or joy of life, has an enormous preventive and healing effect.

Third, if you don't believe in something, your behavior is without a code to guide it. As de Montaigne said, "The wind blows in favor of the ship that has a destination."

Commitment to the destiny for which you were created calls for self-examination. What precisely is your destiny? Commitment to this destiny calls for self-commitment. That sense of calling and inner persuasion sets the level of your priorities, the kinds of stress you will feel responsible to accept, and the kinds you will choose to shrug off as inconsequential. This commitment lets you know when to stand and fight and when to walk away.

Your commitment in life may be to create and maintain friends, to introduce them to one another. You may be committed to maintaining the kind of comradeship and tenderness with your spouse so that the two of you together will be effective and consistent parents. You may be committed to the creation and sustenance of institutions and agencies for the spiritual upbuilding of your family and your neighbors' families. These might include your church, a family and children's agency, or a school for handicapped children. You may be committed to your union and the establishment of just relationships in your company. You may be committed to your profession as a teacher, a lawyer, a physician, or a pastor, and to the sterling practice of that profession. The beliefs underlying these commitments enable you to "take the gaff" of the stress such practices may impose. If you are in activities or situations that you are uncommitted to, your yoke is indeed difficult and your burden is heavy. You have ten times the stress you should be having and your morale is chronically low.

Yet, if any *one* of these commitments is your sole commitment, that one will become an idol to you. Your primary commitment to God saves you from this idolatry. When you lose someone in your family, or when any of your other commitments go sour because of factors beyond your control, then your central commitment to God alone holds you together. The first commandment is to love God. After that, the next commandment is to love our neighbor as well as we do ourselves. In these two commandments is the great secret of managing stress, bearing one another's burdens, and carrying our own loads.

— 7 —

When Stress Completely Overwhelms You

Even the psalmist said, "My heart is in anguish within me, the terrors of death have fallen upon me. Fear and trembling come upon me and horror overwhelms me" (Ps. 55:4–5). He wanted the wings of a dove so that he might fly away and be at rest. You have times when the stresses of life overwhelm you. In military combat, there is an apt phrase: our position is overrun.

There are developmental stresses in life, grief-strickening stresses, and the stresses of increased responsibility. However, such stresses often fade into the background when catastrophic stresses occur, even though they are collective and not individual stresses unless we are directly involved. The 1929 stock market crash, the outbreak of World War II, the unremitting indecision and confusion of the Korean War, the Vietnam War, and the Iranian hostage crisis are examples of such stress. On a less pandemic scale, a hurricane, a tornado, or a massive fire are disasters that are catastrophic. They are all situations in life that may make you want to fly away to be at rest.

One of the strengths that comes to you in such crises is the comradeship and mutuality of suffering you share with a large number of people. The fellowship of hardship, the bonding of people in a common cause, brings out human strengths that hitherto lay dormant and unused. Admittedly this is a bonding which springs from necessity and not from personal choice. But forced cooperation can offer the pattern for later self-chosen collaboration.

In your personal life, however, you may find that a major catastrophe such as I have just described is not the way in which you are overwhelmed by stress. Nor would you have any large community of other sufferers to say, "I know exactly how you feel!" In a very short time, personal stresses can pile up, compound, and exacerbate the feeling of being stressed. You cannot organize your resistance to one event before the alarm of a new stress comes upon you. For example, a person may suffer the loss of a job, a damaging set of rumors as to whether he or she is an honest person, the death of a beloved parent, and the permanent injury and handicap of a son in an auto accident—all within the scope of two months. The drama of Job's overwhelming sufferings is repeated often, even in our day. You may be one of those, like him, who is faced with rebuilding from the ruins of your life.

What are some specific steps to take when you are overwhelmed by stress? Let me enumerate some.

First, consult a physician about the possible impact on your health. Tell him or her what you are going through. Ask for advice about how you should be seeing to it that you stay well. Staying well requires that you get enough sleep, eat properly, take adequate fluids, and have the energy to cope with your life situation.

Second, if you are having trouble doing your work, examine the vacation and sick leave time available to you. You may or may not consider your employer and/ or supervisor a close personal friend but you can simply request a day or a week away in which you can attend to some personal and family business that is pressing. Only you can decide how much of what is happening to you is appropriate to share with the people with whom you work. One word of caution: at least some of the people you work with are competitors for your position, place, recognition, and power. Therefore, choose your confidant carefully. It is not paranoia to recognize the wisdom suggested here as valid.

At any rate, work out some time when you can lighten the stress of the job while you fall back and regroup in order to manage the stresses now overwhelming you. You probably do have close and intimate work associates who will cover for you while you cope with the pressures which are now too much. If you are the kind of person who helps other people a lot, you may frustrate them when they try to help you. The two characteristics often go together. Let others do a few things for you for a change. They will appreciate a chance to do so.

Third, get some time and find a place of privacy so that you can be alone. Job did this and the Lord "answered him out of the whirlwind." Think of yourself as a very complex musical instrument, perhaps a four-manual pipe organ. Think of your emotions as varied and as capable of meaning as the endless combinations of chords, notes, and instruments of that organ. Then, take your Bible and start reading each of the psalms separately. You will find in these psalms the words that give expression to your feelings. Anger, rage, despair, perplexity, exhaustion, suspicion, self-pity, the desire to run from it all, doubt, affirmation of faith, love, praise, relief, joy, peace, and celebration are found there. Yet, they are all lived out in relation to God. The Psalms present God as knowing our thoughts even before we do and affirming them as real, legitimate, and open for expression in prayer. You cannot, by repressing your darkest feelings from God, add to God's knowledge of you. You can, by allowing those dark feelings to surface and be acknowledged, increase the honesty, intimacy, and fellowship with God. Such openness will put your stress picture on a larger canvas. Your perspective will enlarge. Your judgment will improve. Your grip on yourself will be strengthened by the indwelling power of the spirit of God.

Fourth, reach back to comforting rituals from your past and reenact them. I find that a comforting ritual of mine is to repair things that are broken. I come from a family of blue-collar workers. We did not buy new things; we fixed old ones. Now, when the pressure gets too great, I find great solace—and the opportunity to see tangible results—when I set myself to fixing broken lamps, small appliances, cracked windows, and such things. Often, as I do these things, creative solutions to stress problems come to me which I had not seen before.

Fifth, seek the company of young people and little children. Immerse yourself in their concerns. Capture some of their openness, zest, and even naivete about life. To see how little money an adolescent gets for his or her work, to try to answer the question of a four-year-old about why the sun comes up or how much the whole earth costs, reduces your stress by putting it into an unusual relationship with the concerns of youth and children. I know that when I am overwhelmed by stress, a walk with my grandchildren or a Saturday morning breakfast splurge with donuts increases my energy, strengthens my resistance, and lowers my alarm at the stress events besetting me.

Sixth, drop out of sight for a whole day. I could do this by leaving my city of Louisville and driving seventy miles to Lexington, Kentucky, to see a new art exhibit on display at the fine arts center there. Or I could drop out of sight by taking my car to be tuned, have the antifreeze changed, and the transmission serviced at a small garage in another part of my city. There is a small restaurant nearby where I could eat my lunch, read, just stare at the wall, and be blissfully ignored as a stranger. Yet another possibility could be to get lost for a day in a library at a school other than the one at which I teach.

Having some time to yourself to mull over your life situation makes things more bearable. It is like "a rest along the way from the burning of the noontide heat and the burden of the day." From the solitude you capture for yourself, you can gain a kind of renewal of your real destiny in the world. God has started a good work in you and will go on completing it in spite of the stresses that have accumulated around you.

Finally, do not underestimate how multiple stresses within a short period of time can crowd your awareness and impair your decision-making ability. A very important thing to do is have someone who is not too involved in your stresses converse with you on a regular basis. A pastoral counselor is an unusually helpful listener, coach, and confidant with whom to talk. It is good general advice to defer major decisions, especially those that ask for additional stress, until you are well past some of the stresses that are already inundating you. A pastoral counselor can help you sort out the stresses, establish an order of priorities for dealing with them, and provide spiritual direction for the ethical issues you are facing.

If you do not have a pastoral counselor to whom you can turn, you can write to The American Association of Pastoral Counselors, 3000 Connecticut Avenue, N.W., Suite 300, Washington, DC 20008. They can provide you with names, addresses, and telephone numbers of certified pastoral counselors near you. The ideal person would be the pastor of your own church if you feel comfortable in conferring with him or her. Parish pastors, priests, and rabbis are in many instances educated in pastoral counseling, crisis intervention, and stress-relief work. It may well be that you already have such a pastor. Yet it may be that you think he or she is too busy, that there are more needy people than you, or that you are just one in hundreds seen and that you don't want to bother him or her. I have had all these things said about me and have heard them repeatedly from people about their pastors. My strong encouragement to you is to lay such thinking aside, pick up your telephone, and call your pastor. Then, again, all this may be unnecessary for your pastor may have already called you! I hope so.

Your church, especially its small group life of Sunday School classes, weekday Bible study groups, or prayer groups, has as members sincere, well-disciplined people who are acquainted with stress. Many of them are veterans at bearing stress. Joining with them will help you to fulfill the law of Christ, that you love one another as he has loved you and given himself for you.

In the Roman Catholic faith, the saints are specifically designated for special tasks in caring for people. In the Letter of Jude St. Jude cares for people who are in desperate straits, in difficult situations that feel unbearable. In conclusion, I want to pray for you Jude's benediction:

> *Now to him who is able to keep you from falling and to present you without blemish before the presence of his glory with rejoicing, to the only God, Our Saviour through Jesus Christ, be glory, dominion, and authority, before all time, now and forever. Amen.*

Suggestions for Further Reading

Bourne, Peter G., M.D. *Men, Stress, and Vietnam*. Boston: Little, Brown & Co., 1970.

Campbell, Ernest. *Where Cross the Crowded Ways of Life*. New York: Association Press, 1973. (Paperback)

Friedman, Meyer, and Rosenman, Ray H. *Type-A Behavior and Your Heart*. New York: Alfred A. Knopf, 1974. (Paperback)

McQuade, Walter, and Aikman, Ann. *Stress: What It Is; What It Can Do to Your Health; How to Fight Back*. New York: E.P. Dutton Inc., 1974.

Oates, Wayne E. *Confessions of a Workaholic*. Nashville: Abingdon Press, 1978.

Oates, Wayne E. *Nurturing Silence in a Noisy Heart*. New York: Doubleday & Co., Inc., 1979.

Oates, Wayne E. *Workaholics: Make Laziness Work for You*. Nashville: Abingdon Press, 1978. (Paperback)

Oates, Wayne E. *Your Particular Grief*. Philadelphia: Westminster Press, 1981.

Price, Eugenia. *No Pat Answers*. New York: Bantam Books, 1980. (Paperback)

Selye, Hans. *Stress. Without Distress*. New York: J.B. Lippincott Co., 1974.

Selye, Hans. *The Stress of Life*. Revised Edition. New York: McGraw-Hill, 1976.

Steere, Douglas V. *On Being Present Where You Are*. Wallingford, Pennsylvania: Pendle Hill Publications, 1977. (Paperback)